DIA DE LOS MUERTOS

DIA DE LOS MUERTOS IS CELEBRATED ON NOVEMBER 1. AND ENDS ON NOVEMBER 2ND. ALSO KNOWN AS DAY OF THE DEAD, IT IS A CELEBRATION ORIGINATING FROM ANCIENT AZTEC CULTURE BACK IN THE 1500'S. IT IS CELEBRATED IN MEXICO, AND LATIN AMERICAN CULTURES. FAMILIES COME TOGETHER TO CELEBRATE, PRAY, AND HONOR THEIR DECEASED LOVED ONES. THEY HONOR THEM WITH SHRINES, AND ALTARS WITH MANY OF THE DEPARTED FAVORITE ITEMS.

CALAVERAS OR SUGAR SKULLS ARE COMMON FESTIVE DECORATIONS. OFTEN FOUND IN MASKS, OR IN FACE PAINTNG. MARIGOLDS ALSO CELEBRATE DIA DE LOS MUERTO. THEY REPRESENT A PATHWAY THAT GUIDES THE SPIRITS TO THEIR OFFERINGS.

DIA DE LOS MUERTOS IS NOT A SAD DAY, BUT RATHER A CELABRATION OF THE DEAD, WHO WATCH OVER THE LOVED ONES.

DIA DE LOS MUERTOS

CALAVERA

DIA DE LOS MUERTOS

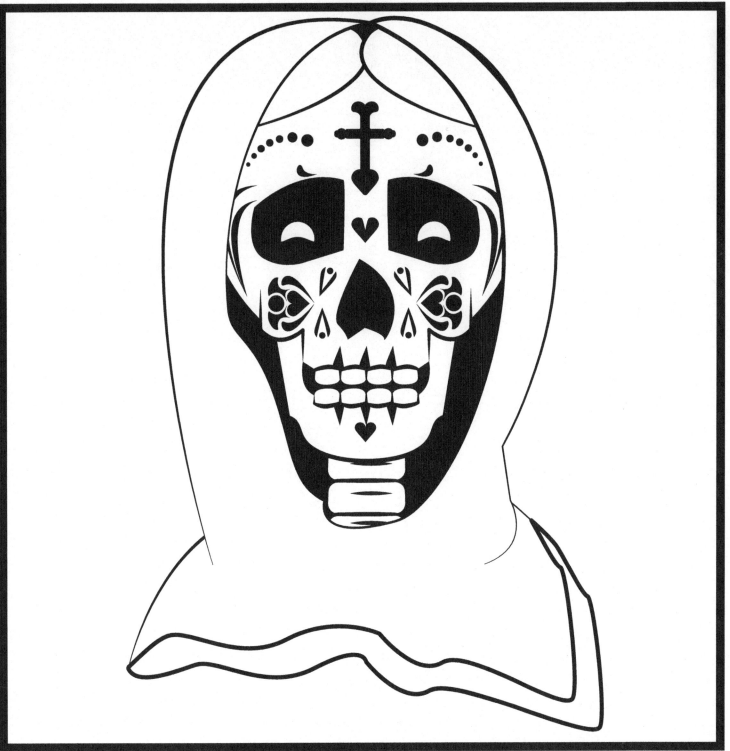

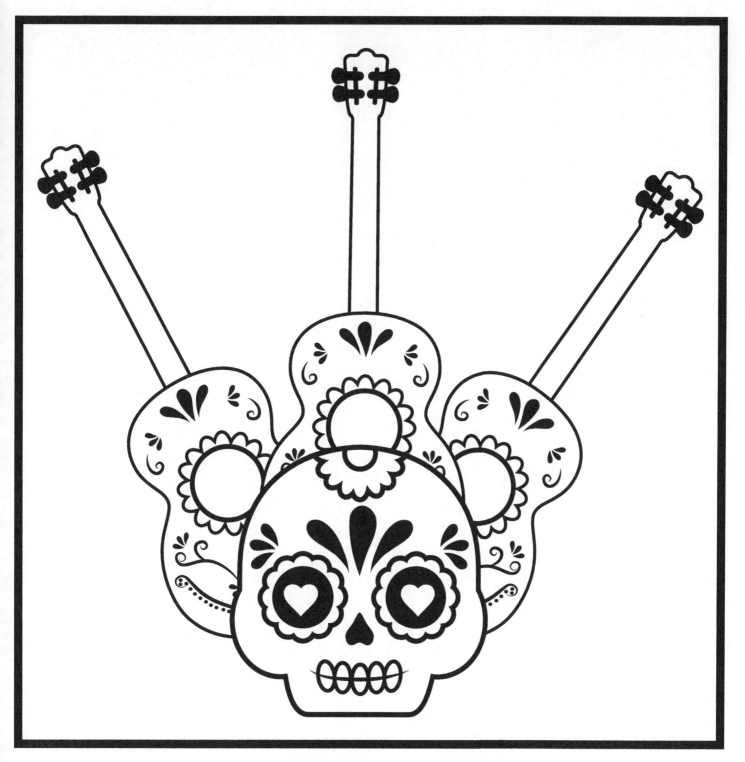

DIA*DE*LOS
MUERTOS

Made in the USA
Middletown, DE
27 September 2022

11397092R00057